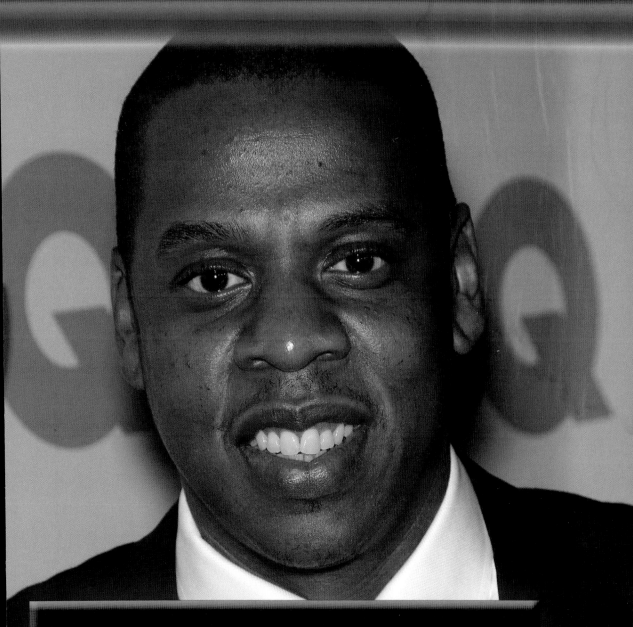

Jay-Z

by C.F. Earl

Superstars of Hip-Hop

Jay-Z

by C.F. Earl

Mason Crest

Jay-Z

Mason Crest
370 Reed Road
Broomall, Pennsylvania 19008
www.masoncrest.com

Printed and bound in the United States of America.

First printing
9 8 7 6 5 4 3 2 1

Library of Congress Cataloging-in-Publication Data

Earl, C. F.
  Jay-Z / C.F. Earl.
      p. cm. – (Superstars of hip hop)
  Includes index.
  ISBN 978-1-4222-2520-2 (hardcover) – ISBN 978-1-4222-2508-0 (series hardcover) – ISBN 978-1-4222-2546-2 (softcover) – ISBN 978-1-4222-9222-8 (ebook)
  1. Jay-Z, 1969--Juvenile literature. 2. Rap musicians–United States–Biography–Juvenile literature. I. Title.
  ML3930.J38E27 2012
  782.421649092–dc22
  [B]
                              2011005807

Produced by Harding House Publishing Services, Inc.
www.hardinghousepages.com
Interior Design by MK Bassett-Harvey.
Cover design by Torque Advertising & Design.

Publisher's notes:
- All quotations in this book come from original sources and contain the spelling and grammatical inconsistencies of the original text.
- The Web sites mentioned in this book were active at the time of publication. The publisher is not responsible for Web sites that have changed their addresses or discontinued operation since the date of publication. The publisher will review and update the Web site addresses each time the book is reprinted.

DISCLAIMER: The following story has been thoroughly researched, and to the best of our knowledge, represents a true story. While every possible effort has been made to ensure accuracy, the publisher will not assume liability for damages caused by inaccuracies in the data, and makes no warranty on the accuracy of the information contained herein. This story has not been authorized nor endorsed by Jay-Z.

Contents

Hip-Hop lingo

Cocaine is an illegal drug that makes a person's senses feel numb.

Someone who is **addicted** to something cannot stop using or doing that thing, even though he may want to.

A **mentor** is a person who teaches someone else life lessons.

To **freestyle** means to make up raps off the top of your head as you perform them.

A **manager** is someone who helps and guides a musician.

Scholarships are money given to pay for a student's education.

Artists are people who create something. Some artists use their voices to make music.

Chapter 1

Shawn from Marcy

On September 14, 2010, Jay-Z stood in front of a sold-out Yankee Stadium. The crowd bounced up and down to the beat, colored lights flashing on their faces. Jay was playing all his biggest hits. He'd been making music for more than fifteen years. And he had plenty of hits to play.

Jay had become one of the biggest names in rap. He'd come up from the bottom. Now he was rapping to packed crowds at Yankee Stadium.

Jay had been called some pretty big names. He'd been called the greatest rapper alive. He'd been called the King of New York. He'd even been called the greatest rapper of all time. Now, standing on stage at Yankee Stadium, he was sure it was all true.

Early Days in Marcy

Jay-Z's real name is Shawn Carter. Shawn was born on December 4, 1970. He was born in Brooklyn, New York.

Shawn was the youngest of four children. His family lived in the Bedford-Stuyvesant neighborhood in Brooklyn. They lived in the Marcy Houses. Marcy was a public housing project in Brooklyn.

When Shawn was eleven, his father left the family. Shawn's mother, Gloria, had to work hard to make money for the family. She worked as a clerk at an investment company.

Shawn was very hurt when his father left. He had looked up to his father. He loved his father. But now he was gone. Gloria made sure to give her son love and support. But Shawn was still hurt by his father.

Shawn could be a show-off when he was young. He liked to do things to get people's attention. His neighbors in Marcy called him "Jazzy." Soon, that name would be shortened to "Jay-Z."

Dealing Drugs

Marcy was a tough place to grow up. Like the Carters, many people in Marcy were poor. Some people turned to drugs to get away from their troubles. Others saw that by selling those drugs, they could make lots of money.

While Shawn was growing up, a new drug was becoming more popular in cities in America. It was called crack. Crack was a kind of **cocaine**. It was a crystal that people smoked.

Crack was much cheaper than cocaine. That meant it was easy for poor people to afford. Many became **addicted** to the drug. They grew to need it. Often, crack ruined the lives of the people who used it.

Crack did many terrible things to cities in America. But selling it was a way to make money. And that meant lots of people sold drugs, no matter how bad it was.

Shawn saw young people around him making money. He saw that selling drugs could help you get the things you wanted. In

Marcy, there weren't many better choices. Especially for poor young people.

Later in his life, Jay-Z told an interviewer, "There was no other way." But selling drugs was dangerous. Shawn had seen his friends die. He'd seen others go to jail. Shawn was smart enough to know that selling drugs was a dead end.

"I got my MBA from Marcy Projects," says Shawn Carter in this sneaker advertisement. The rapper was apparently referring to the business skills he learned while selling drugs in the projects. Although being a dealer was lucrative, Shawn found that it could also be dangerous.

Shawn had an unusual skill at composing rhymes in his head without writing them down. He soon developed this ability, and was able to memorize entire songs, a feat that amazed people involved in the music industry who heard him rapping.

Making Plans

Shawn had always loved music. He loved hip-hop and rap most of all. Shawn had talent for rap, too.

While Shawn was hanging out in Marcy, he'd make rhymes. But he never wrote anything down. Shawn had a talent for keeping lines and verses in his head. Soon, he could think up and remember whole songs.

Shawn started to think rap might be something worth doing for a living. He knew he was good. He was starting to think he could be better than the other rappers. He thought he could even be the best.

Shawn started rapping more and more. People started paying attention. Rapper Jaz-O heard Shawn rap. The two became friends. Jaz-O became Shawn's **mentor**.

Jaz taught Shawn about the music business. Jaz helped Shawn focus on music.

Shawn started calling himself Jay-Z. He took the name from his nickname in Marcy—Jazzy. He also got the name from the J/Z subway lines that stopped in his neighborhood. The name was also like Jaz-O's, Jay's good friend.

Soon, Jay was rapping on Jaz-O's songs. He even got to rap on a song by famous rapper Big Daddy Kane. Jay was meeting lots of new people. And he was just starting out!

Big Daddy Kane started to have Jay **freestyle** at his shows. While Big Daddy Kane took breaks to change his clothes, Jay would come out and keep the crowd going. It was a great way to have more people see Jay rap.

Then Jay met Damon Dash. Dash was the man who would help Jay become a star.

A New Hustle

Damon Dash was a music **manager** from Harlem, New York. He also helped to plan big parties. Dash grew up going to good schools on **scholarships**.

In 1995 Damon "Dame" Dash offered to manage Jay-Z's music career. Dash was a shrewd businessman and entrepreneur who had a plan to develop a hip-hop music and fashion empire. He considered Shawn a talented performer who could help him promote various products and interests.

Dash learned to be a good businessman. To make money, he threw parties in the early 1990s. Then, he'd put that money into his music management business.

Dash had a dream for a business based around hip-hop. He wanted his business to mix music and fashion.

Dash's idea was to make money on everything about hip-hop. He planned to make music with new **artists**. Then, those artists would wear and talk about his clothing. Dash wanted to sell hip-hop fans both music and clothes. He wanted to sell them the entire hip-hop image.

At first, Dash did some rapping to get the word out about his business. Soon, he learned he needed a better rapper to be the face of his business, though. That was around the time he met Jay-Z.

Dash liked Jay's flow. Jay was a talented rapper. Dash knew they could be good partners. Dash became Jay's manager.

Jay knew he had finally escaped from his old life.

Hip-Hop lingo

An **album** is a group of songs collected together on a CD.

A **producer** is the person in charge of putting together songs. A producer makes the big decisions about the music.

Beats are the basic rhythms or pulse of a piece of music.

A **record label** is a company that produces music for singers and groups and puts out CDs.

Master recordings are the original recordings made by artists. The vocals, beats, and other pieces are then mixed together from the master recordings to make the final track of a song. Artists almost never own their master recordings or have any control over them.

An **executive producer** makes the business decisions about an album and sometimes artistic decisions as well.

Pop is short for "popular." Pop music is usually light and happy, with a good beat.

A **single** is a song that is sold by itself.

Lyrics are the words in a song.

The **chorus** is the part of a song that repeats between verses.

Each year, the National Academy of Recording Arts and Sciences gives out the Grammy Awards (short for Gramophone Awards)—or **Grammys**—to people who have done something really big in the music industry.

Critics are people who judge artistic works and say what is good and what is bad about them.

Chapter 2

Brooklyn's Finest

Damon Dash knew Jay-Z was something special. He was excited about Jay's music. He was so excited, he was going to pay to make Jay-Z's first **album**. Dash and Jay also had help from their friend Kareem "Biggs" Burke.

Together, the three started making Jay's first album. It was called *Reasonable Doubt*.

Jay, Dash, and Burke looked for talented rappers and producers to work on the album. Jay's friend DJ Clark Kent became the album's **producer**. Jay and DJ Clark Kent had met while Jay was working with Big Daddy Kane and Jaz-O.

DJ Clark Kent would make many **beats** for *Reasonable Doubt*. DJ Premier also made beats for the album.

The three friends also got Notorious B.I.G. to rap with Jay on the album. Like Jay, B.I.G. was from Brooklyn. Jay and Biggie worked together on the song "Brooklyn's Finest." They became good friends after working together.

Soon, *Reasonable Doubt* was finished. Jay, Dash, and Burke needed to get a record company to sell the album. So, they went to every

record label in New York City. They tried to get someone to put out Jay's album. But no one wanted to. Every company turned them down.

The three friends spent a whole year trying to get a company to take the album. No one did. After that year, they had an idea. If nobody wanted to sell their music, why didn't they sell it themselves?

Damon Dash, Jay-Z, and Biggs Burke are shown together at the Rocawear 2002 Fall Fashion Show in New York City. The three men established the hip-hop music label Roc-A-Fella Records in 1995 to distribute Jay-Z's first album.

Roc-A-Fella Records

So the three started their own record company. They called the company Roc-A-Fella Records. They started Roc-A-Fella in 1996.

Roc-A-Fella started selling *Reasonable Doubt*. The company made deals with other companies to put the album in stores. Soon, Roc-A-Fella had sold 500,000 albums.

It wasn't long before the three friends knew they had something special. They saw that they didn't need to be part of a big record company. Roc-A-Fella could become a big company all by itself. By selling their own music, they could be more successful. They could also keep control over everything.

Roc-A-Fella made a deal with Def Jam Recordings. The two companies decided to split up everything they made from Jay's music evenly. Jay-Z also got to own the **master recordings** of his own music. That was something very new for most rappers. Jay couldn't have done that without Roc-A-Fella behind him.

Things had changed a lot. Before, Jay, Dash, and Burke hadn't gotten any attention from big companies. Now, they had the power. People wanted to work with Jay-Z. Big companies wanted to make deals with him.

With Roc-A-Fella, Jay, Dash, and Burke could do things their own way. It was the best thing for them. And for Jay-Z's music.

A Friend Passes

By 1996, East and West Coast rappers were fighting a lot. They were making songs dissing each other. They were even threatening each other.

Tupac Shakur and Notorious B.I.G. were two of rap's biggest names. Tupac was from the West Coast. Biggie was from the East. It was a battle between Los Angeles and New York. Who had the best rappers? Who sold the most albums?

Jay-Z did not want to be drawn into the rivalry between Tupac (left) and Notorious B.I.G. Jay-Z was friendly with B.I.G., who had contributed vocals to *Reasonable Doubt,* and was saddened when the rapper was murdered in March 1997.

Tupac and Biggie battled in their songs for years. Then, in 1996, Tupac was killed in Las Vegas. A few months later, B.I.G. was killed in Los Angeles. No one knows who killed either Tupac or Biggie.

To many, it was clear that their musical battle had gotten too real. Others think that the rap battle wasn't the real reason they were killed. Nobody knows exactly why they were killed or by whom. One thing is for sure: when Biggie was killed, Jay lost a great friend.

Wearing a bulletproof vest, Jay-Z performs at a concert in Massachusetts in 1997. In his song "Lucky Me," the rapper discusses the price of fame, including his fear that he might be gunned down just as Tupac and Notorious B.I.G. had been.

In My Lifetime, Vol. 1

With Notorious B.I.G. gone, New York had lost its king. He'd been the biggest name in New York rap for years. Now, someone had to take his place.

Jay was very sad about Biggie's death. But he also wanted to be the new King of New York. So, he started working hard on his next album. Jay called his second album *In My Lifetime, Vol. 1.*

Sean "Puffy" Combs was the album's **executive producer**. Some producers that helped on *Reasonable Doubt* also made beats for *In My Lifetime*. DJ Premier worked on both albums.

In My Lifetime had a different sound from *Reasonable Doubt*. Jay's first album had been dark and tough. On it, he'd rapped about the life of a gangster and drug dealer. *In My Lifetime* sounded more like **pop** music. Its beats weren't as dark.

Many fans didn't like this new sound for Jay. They liked to think of Jay-Z as tough and street-smart. They didn't want somebody as hard as Jay-Z to be making pop music.

Def Jam businessmen had wanted Jay's album to have both hard rap and some poppier songs. They wanted to make sure lots of people had a song to like on Jay's new album.

Jay-Z said that his new sound was about showing more of himself. He said that he had more in him than the gangster sound of *Reasonable Doubt*. He wanted to show fans another side of himself.

Even with some fans not liking it, *In My Lifetime* sold more than a million copies. It gave Jay-Z even more fans. It also put him in line to be King of New York.

Vol. 2: Hard Knock Life

In 1998, Jay released his third album. He called it *Vol. 2: Hard Knock Life*. The album followed up *In My Lifetime, Vol. 1.*

The first **single** from the album was called "Hard Knock Life (Ghetto Anthem)." It mixed Jay's hard **lyrics** with a softer pop beat. The song's **chorus** is a sample from the musical *Annie*.

The song was the biggest hit Jay had had yet. The summer it came out, it was one of the biggest songs on radio. With help from "Hard Knock Life," the album was number one right away.

Hard Knock Life had beats from some of the biggest producers in rap. Timbaland, Jus Blaze, and new producer Swizz Beatz worked on the album. DMX and Ja Rule rapped on the album along with others guests. Jaz-O also shows up on *Hard Knock Life*.

Some fans didn't like that most songs on the album had guests. These fans wanted more songs with Jay-Z rapping by himself. Some thought Jay's best songs didn't have guests.

These fans couldn't stop the album from selling, though. *Hard Knock Life* sold more than five million copies. It is one of Jay's best-selling albums.

At the 1999 **Grammys**, Jay won Best Rap Album for *Hard Knock Life*. Jay didn't go to the Awards show, though. He decided that too many other rappers weren't getting the respect they deserved. So Jay didn't go to the show to get his Grammy.

Jay-Z was now one of the biggest rappers in the world. Fans and **critics** respected his music. He'd sold millions of albums. Though he'd lost his friend, B.I.G., he was moving on. Jay was ready to take over the rap world.

Hip-Hop lingo

The **hook** of a song is a short section that catches people's attention. A lot of times, the hook is the chorus, but not always.

A **studio album** is a collection of songs put together in a recording studio.

Someone who **produced** a song decided how to put the music together and made decisions about the kind of beats in a song, how fast it would be, and what kind of sound the song would have.

Something that is **classic** is likely to be popular for a long time.

Chapter 3

Building an Empire

Jay-Z wanted to be more than a rap star. He wanted to use his stardom and music to do more.

Rocawear

In 1999, Roc-A-Fella Records started Rocawear. Rocawear was a clothing company. The company would make the kind of clothes that Jay-Z wore. That way, Rocawear could sell clothes just by having Jay wear them.

Jay's fans wanted to buy his clothes because they wanted to be like him. This was right in line with Damon Dash's plan for Roc-A-Fella. He'd always wanted to make hip-hop a business.

Dash used Jay's music to sell Rocawear clothes. Then he used Rocawear clothes to sell Jay's music. He'd throw parties to sell the clothes. Then, he'd use Jay's music to get people excited to come to the party. This is called "cross-marketing."

Roc-A-Fella started Rocawear at just the right time. Jay-Z had never been more popular. After *Vol. 2: Hard Knock Life*, he was one of the biggest names in rap. With Biggie and Tupac gone, many people thought Jay was the next great rapper.

Vol. 3: The Life and Times of S. Carter

Jay put his next album out on December 28, 1999. He called it *Vol. 3: The Life and Times of S. Carter*. The album was number one the week it came out. It was Jay's second number-one album.

The first single from *The Life and Times of S. Carter* was called "Big Pimpin'." The song had a bouncy pop beat and a catchy **hook**. The hip-hop group UGK joined Jay on the song, too. It was a huge hit.

With the help of "Big Pimpin'," Jay sold three million copies of the album.

Roc-A-Fella was growing, too. The label was signing more artists. Rocawear was becoming more successful. It seemed like Jay was on top of the world.

The Dynasty: Roc La Familia

In 2000, Jay-Z put out *The Dynasty: Roc La Familia*. *The Dynasty* was meant to be an album that showed off the talent of other Roc-A-Fella rappers.

Soon, that plan changed, though. Instead, the album became Jay-Z's fifth **studio album**. It still had lots of Roc-A-Fella guests, but it wasn't the group effort it was meant to be.

The Dynasty was the number-one album in the country when it came out. That made it Jay's third number-one album. It was his second in less than a year.

Jay also wanted to have new producers work on the album. He chose Kanye West, Just Blaze, and the Neptunes to help on *The Dynasty*.

At the time, these producers were just coming up. They weren't as successful as they are today. After *The Dynasty* came out, they all became more famous. More artists wanted to work with them, too. *The Dynasty* gave these producers their first big breaks.

The Dynasty ended up selling more than two million copies.

Jay-Z Against Nas

After Notorious B.I.G. died in 1997, lots of New York rappers wanted to be the new King of New York. Jay-Z was going for the crown, too. He was facing other rappers like DMX, Jadakiss, and Nas. Nas would become Jay's greatest enemy.

The August 2005 issue of *XXL* magazine pictures Jay-Z with members of Roc La Familia, the rapper's associates on the Roc-A-Fella Records label. Jay-Z's 2000 album *The Dynasty: Roc La Familia* was a collaboration that featured many of these up-and-coming performers.

In 2001, rapper Prodigy from Mobb Deep said he thought Jay was trying to insult the group. Later that year, Jay spoke out against Prodigy and Mobb Deep. Then, that summer, Jay performed a song called "Takeover" from his next album. In "Takeover," Jay rapped

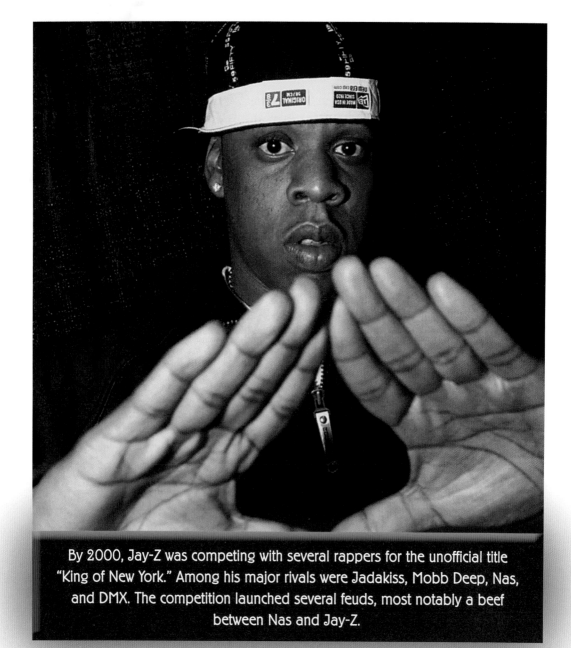

By 2000, Jay-Z was competing with several rappers for the unofficial title "King of New York." Among his major rivals were Jadakiss, Mobb Deep, Nas, and DMX. The competition launched several feuds, most notably a beef between Nas and Jay-Z.

about Mobb Deep, Prodigy, and Nas. Many people thought Nas was as good as Jay-Z. They thought he and Jay were the two rappers closest to being the new King of New York.

Nas heard about Jay's new song dissing him. He recorded a song called "Ether." In "Ether," Nas raps about Jay not respecting Biggie's memory. Jay added another verse to "Takeover" to get back at Nas.

Jay and Nas would go back and forth like this for years. They traded more and more insults in their verses. The battle to be the next King of New York was getting ugly.

The Blueprint

Jay-Z wrote his next album in two days. Then, the album was recorded in just two weeks. It was called *The Blueprint*. Jay released it on September 11, 2001, never knowing what else was going to happen that day. September 11th was the same day that terrorists attacked the United States.

Despite the terrible thing that had happened, *The Blueprint* was the number-one album in the country that week. It sold 427,000 copies in that week, too. Jay's music gave many New Yorkers a place to escape in the sad time after 9/11.

The album was different from Jay-Z's other albums. Instead of having lots of guests, the album had only one song with a guest. Eminem was the only other artist to rap on *The Blueprint*. He also **produced** the song "Renegade."

Kanye West produced four of the songs on *The Blueprint*. This was one of Kanye's first big breaks. Soon, with Jay-Z's help, Kanye would be known for his own music.

The Blueprint had a few big singles. The first single from the album was called "Izzo (H.O.V.A.)." "Girls, Girls, Girls" and "Song Cry" were also big hits for Jay.

YEAR-END SPECIAL // WINNERS & LOSERS

Vibe

NAS & JAY-Z
THE SHOCKING UNION

PLUS: THE OTHER 42 UNFORGETTABLE
MOMENTS OF 2005

Nas and Jay-Z are featured on the cover of the January 2006 issue of *Vibe* magazine. The two rappers ended their feud peacefully in 2005, performing songs together at the "I Declare War" concert sponsored by New York radio station Power 105.1.

Today, many fans and critics believe that *The Blueprint* is a hip-hop **classic**. Many also think it's Jay-Z's best album. It has sold more than three million copies.

The Blueprint 2: The Gift & the Curse

Jay-Z's next album was called *The Blueprint 2: The Gift & the Curse*. It came out on November 12, 2002.

The *Blueprint 2* was two albums in one. The first was called *The Gift*. The second album was called *The Curse*.

The album had two big singles. The first was "Excuse Me Miss." The second was called "'03 Bonnie and Clyde." "Bonnie and Clyde" was the biggest single on the album. Beyoncé sang the hook on the song.

Beyoncé and Jay had been dating for a while by the time "Bonnie and Clyde" came out. They don't like to talk about their relationship. Many people think they started dating in 1999, though. Later, in 2008, they got married.

The album was a big hit. *The Blueprint 2* sold more than three million copies.

In 2003, *The Blueprint 2* was released again. The new version of *The Blueprint 2* was called *The Blueprint 2.1*. This time, it was only one album. Some songs from the first version were left off. Some new songs were added, too.

Jay was also doing more as a businessman. In 2003, Jay opened his first 40/40 Club sports bar in New York. Rocawear started to sell women's and kids' clothes. Reebok even made Jay the first person to have his own shoe who wasn't an athlete. Soon, Jay would leave rap to go after his goals in business full time.

Hip-Hop lingo

A **mash-up** is a song that has been made by blending two or more different songs together.

An album is **leaked** if people start listening to it before it is sold in stores.

A **soundtrack** is a collection of all the songs on a movie.

Chapter 4

Retirement and Return

At the opening of Jay's 40/40 Club in New York, he told fans he was working on another album. Then, he told them that the new album would be his last.

The new album was called *The Black Album*. At first, Jay said that each song would have a different producer. When the album came out, Kanye West, Just Blaze, and the Neptunes each made two beats. Eminem, Rick Rubin, 9th Wonder, Timbaland, and others also produced beats.

The Black Album had a few hit singles. Songs like "Change Clothes," "Dirt Off My Shoulder," "99 Problems," and "What More Can I Say" were all big on the radio.

The Black Album sold more than three million copies. The album was number one the week it came out. It was Jay's ninth number-one album in a row.

Fade to Black

On November 25, 2003, Jay-Z held a concert called Fade to Black. The show was held at Madison Square Garden in New York City. It was meant to be Jay-Z's last concert. He called it his retirement party.

The concert was also going to be filmed. Jay wanted the concert to be made into a movie. He called the movie of the show *Fade to Black*. The movie would show fans the concert and some of Jay's work on *The Black Album*.

At the concert, Jay played all his hit songs. He rapped verses from his first album. He played his newest hits. The concert was for Jay-Z fans. Jay wanted to make sure they liked his last show.

In 2003, Jay-Z announced that proceeds from his 2003 Fade to Black concert would be donated to the Hip-Hop Summit Action Network (HSAN). Pictured here are (left to right) HSAN chairman Russell Simmons and president Dr. Ben Chavis, Jay-Z, rapper Reverend Run, and Memphis Bleek.

In 2004, Jay worked with Linkin Park on *Collision Course*. The album had six songs on it. The songs were parts of Jay's songs with parts of Linkin Park's songs. This type of mixed song is called a **mash-up**. The mash-up album sold more than a million copies.

At the end of 2004, Jay moved on to business. He became president of Def Jam Records. Def Jam bought Roc-A-Fella Records, too. Jay would run both companies.

Jay-Z was at the top of the music world. And now he was stepping down. He'd done it all. It was time for him to do something new. One of the best rappers of all time was done rhyming.

The Return of Jay-Z

Jay began his work at Def Jam in 2005. For months, he focused on his new job. He worked to bring up new artists. He worked to get word out about his artists.

For these months, Jay didn't play shows. He had no plans to put out more music. But, it wasn't long before Jay-Z fans started talking about Jay's return to rap.

In October 2005, Jay-Z played a show called I Declare War in New York. The stage was made to look like the Oval Office. The show was meant to celebrate Jay's new job as the president and CEO of Def Jam.

At the end of the show, Nas joined Jay on stage. Jay and Nas said that their beef was over. They had become friends and gotten over their past battles. Together, they performed a mash-up of Jay's "Dead Presidents" and Nas's "The World is Yours."

Jay was now the president of one of rap's biggest labels. He'd also ended a beef that lasted years. Fans were starting to hear that he might come back to making music, too.

In 2005, Jay-Z took over as president and CEO of Def Jam Recordings. In his new job, he oversees the development of talented new stars for the label. Although he was officially retired from performing, rumors persisted that he might one day release another album.

Kingdom Come

It wasn't long before fans learned that the rumors were true. Jay-Z's comeback album was called *Kingdom Come*. The album came out in November 2006.

The first single from the album was called "Show Me What You Got." The single was **leaked** onto the Internet in October 2006.

Radio stations began to play it a lot. That only made fans more excited for Jay's new album.

When *Kingdom Come* came out, it went to number one. It was Jay's ninth number-one album in a row. The album sold more than 600,000 copies in one week. It was the highest one-week sales for a Jay-Z album.

Kingdom Come was an important album for Jay-Z. He was back. He was rapping again. And fans couldn't be happier to have him.

American Gangster

In November 2007, Jay put out his tenth album. It was called *American Gangster*. The album was based on Jay seeing Ridley Scott's movie *American Gangster.* The album sold more than a million copies.

The album wasn't meant to be the **soundtrack** to the movie. Instead, it was an album about how the film's characters and Jay's lives were the same in many ways. Jay used the movie as a starting place, but then built on it using his own life.

At the end of 2007, Jay-Z said he would step down as president of Def Jam. He said he'd leave his job as president and CEO in 2008. As an artist, Jay stayed with Def Jam. On January 1, 2008, Jay left his job at Def Jam.

Hip-Hop lingo

A **duet** is a song performed by two people.

Tracks are parts—usually songs—of an album.

A **tour** is when a person travels around and plays music for people at concerts.

If you **inspire** people, you make them want to do something and make them feel good about themselves.

Chapter 5

The King of New York

Jay-Z has done more in business than almost any other rapper. He's always been a hard worker. He took the drive that made him so successful and put it into business. He helped make Roc-A-Fella a big name in rap. Rocawear became a famous company with his help. Jay's skills in business make him more than just another rapper.

Today, Jay is working on many different projects. His new company, Roc Nation, does lots of different things in music. They help artists record. They sell the albums. They also spread the word about new music. Jay says he wants to give new artists the chances he never had.

Jay also produced a Broadway musical called *Fela!* with Will Smith and Jada Pinkett. The musical is based on the life of musician Fela Kuti. The show was a big hit on Broadway with fans and critics.

Jay-Z also started the 40/40 Club. The club is an expensive sports bar. He's got 40/40 Clubs in New York, Atlanta, and Chicago. Jay even has plans for 40/40 Clubs in Tokyo and Singapore.

Jay even owns part of the New Jersey Nets basketball team. The Nets moved to Jay-Z's hometown, Brooklyn, New York, for the 2012-2013 season. The Nets also changed their name to become The Brooklyn Nets.

Jay-Z shows off the four awards he received at the 2004 MTV Video Music Awards ceremony in Miami. He won awards for Best Rap Video, Best Direction in a Video, Best Editing, and Best Cinematography.

Jay-Z's businesses are huge successes. The rapper has made millions by making smart decisions. He's chosen what he wants to work on. Jay is one of the few rappers who have had lots of success in business as well as rap.

The Blueprint 3

The Blueprint 3 came out on September 8, 2009. It was Jay-Z's eleventh studio album.

The album was meant to come out on September 11, 2009. It would have been eight years since the first *Blueprint* came out. But fans wanted the new album so much that the date was moved up a few days.

The Blueprint 3 was the number-one album in the country when it came out. That made it Jay's eleventh number-one album in a row. Elvis Presley used to be the record holder. Now, Jay-Z had more number-one albums than the King.

The first single from *Blueprint 3* was called "D.O.A. (Death of Auto-Tune)." Other songs from the album, like "Young Forever" and "Run This Town," were big hits. Rhianna sings the hook on "Run This Town." Kanye West raps a verse in the song, too.

The biggest hit from *The Blueprint 3* was "Empire State of Mind." The song was a **duet** between Jay-Z and Alicia Keys. Keys sung the chorus and Jay rapped the verses. The song was a huge success for both artists.

Kanye West produced most of *The Blueprint 3*. Timbaland, the Neptunes, and No I.D. also produced **tracks** for the album.

The Blueprint 3 was released on Jay's new label Roc Nation. Jay didn't want to stay with Def Jam after *Kingdom Come* and *American Gangster*. Instead, he wanted to go out on his own. *The Blueprint 3* was Jay's last album in the *Blueprint* series.

The album sold almost half a million copies in its first week. Over the next year, *The Blueprint 3* sold more than three million copies.

Home and Home Tour

In 2010, Jay-Z started the Home and Home **Tour** with Eminem. The two rappers are among the biggest stars in hip-hop. Both have been making music for more than ten years.

In May of that year, Jay-Z and Eminem announced the tour at a baseball game. The game was between the Detroit Tigers and the New York Yankees. With Jay from New York and Eminem from Detroit, it was perfect.

They said the tour had only two stops. First, Jay and Eminem would play in Detroit. They'd play at the Detroit Tigers stadium. Next, the two would perform in New York. They'd be playing at Yankee Stadium. They would play two shows in each city.

Jay-Z's part of the concerts was about looking back on his life. He played songs from his earlier albums.

Jay even rapped a few of Notorious B.I.G,'s songs. Jay-Z wanted to pay his respects to his friend. Jay-Z is keeping Biggie's memory alive.

The Home and Home Tour showed that, like Biggie, Jay-Z is a **legend** in New York.

Decoded

On November 16, 2010 Jay-Z released his first book. The book was called *Decoded*.

Jay wanted his book to be different. He didn't want his book to just be the story of his life. He wanted it to tell fans who he was. He wanted to let people in on what made Shawn Carter into Jay-Z.

The book focuses on Jay's lyrics. He wanted fans to understand his songs better. With the book, fans have a chance to see into Jay's mind. They can learn more about how he comes up with his verses.

On Top of the World

Jay had a big year in 2011. He and Kanye West released an album called *Watch the Throne*. Together, the two rap superstars couldn't fail. The album was a huge hit, reaching number one on the charts in its first week. The two rappers toured together after releasing *Watch the Throne*. The tour, like the album, was a bit hit with fans!

Jay found out that he was going to be a father in 2011, too. In January, 2012, Beyonce gave birth to daughter Blue Ivy Carter in New York City. She and Jay-Z couldn't have been happier.

Just a few days later, Jay released a song called "Glory." In the song, he raps about how happy he is to be a father. At the end of "Glory," Jay recorded Blue Ivy crying. He told fans that it was the beginning of her music career. When "Glory" became a hit on the Billboard charts, Blue Ivy Carter became the youngest person ever on the charts!

Looking to the Future

Jay-Z has shown the world there isn't much he can't do. He's one of the most famous rappers of all time. He's a successful business-man, too. He's married to Beyoncé, one of pop music's top artists. His name is known around the world.

Shawn Carter from Marcy Projects has become one of America's biggest stars. Today, Jay-Z has more number-one albums than Elvis Presley. Many believe he is one of the greatest rappers ever to pick up a mic.

Jay-Z's life in music has been bigger and better than almost any other artist's. His life and his music **inspire** millions of fans around the world. Jay will keep working hard to give his fans what they want. His drive to succeed has taken him this far. Where it will take him next is up to him.

1970 Shawn Carter is born on December 4 to Gloria Carter and Adnis Reeves in Brooklyn, New York.

1982 Adnis Reeves leaves the family home, an event Shawn would later cite as part of the reason he turned to the streets.

1988 Shawn, a neighborhood drug dealer, distinguishes himself as a talented rapper. He records "Hawaiian Sophie" and a video for "The Originators" with Jaz-O, a more established rapper who helps show him the business.

1994 Jay steps into the limelight with superstar rapper Big Daddy Kane, recording a video for "Show and Prove." He continues to hustle drugs.

1995 Jay meets Damon Dash, who signs him to a management deal. They begin to look for a record deal for Jay together.

1996 Jay, Dash, and another associate, Kareem Burke, contribute funds to form Roc-A-Fella Records. Jay's funds come from close to six years of drug sales. Reasonable Doubt is released. The album goes gold and will ultimately be hailed as a hip-hop classic. Roc-A-Fella begins negotiations with Def Jam.

1997 Jay's friend Notorious B.I.G. is murdered in Los Angeles. Def Jam and Roc-A-Fella agree to a joint venture, and *In My Lifetime, Vol. 1* is released. The album does well commercially and signifies a move toward a pop audience. Jay retires from the drug business.

1998 Jay releases his biggest hit to date, *Vol. 2: Hard Knock Life*. It will eventually sell more than 5 million copies. He also embarks on a 52-city tour of the same name. Roc-A-Fella Records branches into fashion with the launch of the urban fashion house Rocawear.

1999   Jay releases *Vol. 3: Life and Times of S. Carter*, which garners more critical acclaim than *Vol. 2*. In December, Jay is on hand at a New York nightclub when Lance "Un" Rivera is stabbed. He is charged with the stabbing but denies involvement.

2000   *The Dynasty: Roc La Familia*, a compilation album featuring many Roc-A-Fella artists, is released. It sells well but is a critical failure. Jay accepts a plea agreement to avoid jail for his role in Un's stabbing.

2001   Jay releases *The Blueprint* on September 11, the same morning that terrorist attacks level the World Trade Center and damage the Pentagon. He performs "Izzo (H.O.V.A.)," a single from the album, at the charity event, The Concert for New York. He also impresses listeners with an MTV Unplugged performance, backed by players from hip-hop group The Roots.

2002   Jay releases his first double disc, *The Blueprint 2*. It goes quadruple platinum.

2003   *The Black Album* is released with much fanfare, as it is Jay-Z's final album. The concert he plans as a good-bye sells out Madison Square Garden in less than 5 minutes. "99 Problems," a single from the album, wins a Grammy. It sells well and is generally well accepted in both hip-hop and pop circles. Jay-Z "retires" from his career officially, but he continues making records and touring.

2004   Adnis Reeves reconciles with his son. Jay begins negotiations with Warner Music Group and Def Jam Recordings, both of which are offering him an executive post. Jay embarks on tour with R. Kelly, only to have the tour fall apart. Kelly eventually sues him for $75 million. The suit has not been resolved.

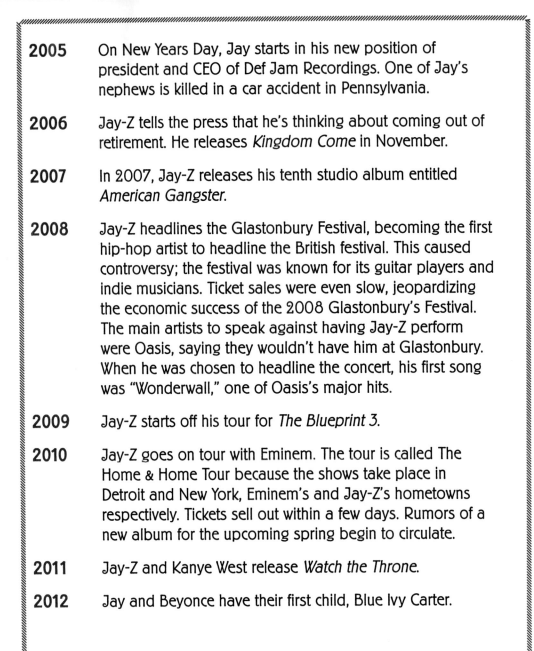

2005   On New Years Day, Jay starts in his new position of president and CEO of Def Jam Recordings. One of Jay's nephews is killed in a car accident in Pennsylvania.

2006   Jay-Z tells the press that he's thinking about coming out of retirement. He releases *Kingdom Come* in November.

2007   In 2007, Jay-Z releases his tenth studio album entitled *American Gangster*.

2008   Jay-Z headlines the Glastonbury Festival, becoming the first hip-hop artist to headline the British festival. This caused controversy; the festival was known for its guitar players and indie musicians. Ticket sales were even slow, jeopardizing the economic success of the 2008 Glastonbury's Festival. The main artists to speak against having Jay-Z perform were Oasis, saying they wouldn't have him at Glastonbury. When he was chosen to headline the concert, his first song was "Wonderwall," one of Oasis's major hits.

2009   Jay-Z starts off his tour for *The Blueprint 3*.

2010   Jay-Z goes on tour with Eminem. The tour is called The Home & Home Tour because the shows take place in Detroit and New York, Eminem's and Jay-Z's hometowns respectively. Tickets sell out within a few days. Rumors of a new album for the upcoming spring begin to circulate.

2011   Jay-Z and Kanye West release *Watch the Throne*.

2012   Jay and Beyonce have their first child, Blue Ivy Carter.

Discography
Albums

1996	Reasonable Doubt
1997	In My Lifetime, Vol. 1
1998	Vol. 2: Hard Knock Life
1999	Vol. 3: Life and Times of S. Carter
2000	The Dynasty: Roc La Familia
2001	The Blueprint
	Jay-Z: Unplugged
2002	The Best of Both Worlds (with R. Kelly)
	The Blueprint 2: The Gift & the Curse
2003	The Blueprint 2.1
	The Black Album
2004	Unfinished Business (with R. Kelly)
	Collision Course (with Linkin Park)
2006	Kingdom Come
2007	American Gangster
2009	The Blueprint 3
2011	Watch the Throne (with Kanye West)

In Books

Baker, Soren. *The History of Rap and Hip Hop*. San Diego, Calif.: Lucent, 2006.

Comissiong, Solomon W. F. *How Jamal Discovered Hip-Hop Culture*. New York: Xlibris, 2008.

Cornish, Melanie. *The History of Hip Hop*. New York: Crabtree, 2009.

Czekaj, Jef. *Hip and Hop, Don't Stop!* New York: Hyperion, 2010.

Haskins, Jim. *One Nation Under a Groove: Rap Music and Its Roots*. New York: Jump at the Sun, 2000.

Hatch, Thomas. *A History of Hip-Hop: The Roots of Rap*. Portsmouth, N.H.: Red Bricklearning, 2005.

Websites

Def Jam Records
www.defjam.com

Island Def Jam
www.rocafella.com

Jay-Z on Myspace
www.myspace.com/jayz

The Official Jay-Z Website
www.jay-z.com/index.php

Index

Index

About the Author

C.F. Earl is a writer living and working in Binghamton, New York. Earl writes mostly on social and historical topics, including health, the military, and finances. An avid student of the world around him, and particularly fascinated with almost any current issue, C.F. Earl hopes to continue to write for books, websites, and other publications for as long as he is able.

Picture Credits

Def Jam Records/NMI: p. 14, 22
Djamilla/Big Pictures USA: p. 16
Dreamstime.com, Sbukley: p. 1
Feature Photo Service/NMI: p. 9, 34
FWD Photos/George De Sota: p. 6
KRT/NMI: p. 36
Michelle Feng/NMI: p. 28
PRNewsFoto/NMI: pp. 12, 30, 32, 38
WENN: p. 25
Zuma Press/Jane Caine: p. 18 (right)
Zuma Press/Steven Tackeff: pp. 10, 19, 26
Zuma Press/Toronto Star: p. 18 (left)

To the best knowledge of the publisher, all other images are in the public domain. If any image has been inadvertently uncredited, please notify Harding House Publishing Services, Vestal, New York 13850, so that rectification can be made for future printings.